CROWN FINANCIAL MINISTRIES

Discovering God's Way Of Handling MONEY

A FINANCIAL STUDY FOR TEENS

By Howard and Bev Dayton

LEADER'S GUIDE

ISBN 1-56427-034-3

Verses identified as KJV are taken from the King James Version.

Verses identified as NIV are taken from the *Holy Bible: New International Version*, copyright 1973, 1978, 1984 by the International Bible Society. Used by permission of Zondervan Bible Publishers.

Verses identified as AMPLIFIED are from the *Amplified New Testament*, copyright 1954, 1958, 1987 by the Lockman Foundation. Used by permission.

Verses identified as TLB are taken from *The Living Bible*, copyright 1971 by Tyndale House Publishers, Wheaton, IL. Used by permission.

All other verses are taken from the *New American Standard Bible®* (Updated Edition), copyright 1960, 1962, 1963, 1968, 1971, 1972, 1973, 1975, 1977, 1995 by The Lockman Foundation. Used by permission.

June 2005 Edition

Contents

Objectives/Leader's Responsibilities

Objectives of the Study

1.) Encourage the students to experience more intimate fellowship with Christ.

Luke 16:11 expresses the correlation between how we handle our resources and the quality of our fellowship with the Lord: *"Therefore if you have not been faithful in the use of worldly* wealth, who will entrust the true riches to you?"* For some students, this study may be their first opportunity to learn about Jesus Christ.

2.) Challenge each person to acknowledge Jesus Christ as Lord.

Money is a primary competitor with Christ for the lordship of our lives. In Matthew 6:24 Jesus says, *"No one can serve two masters; for either he will hate the one and love the other, or he will be devoted to one and despise the other. You cannot serve God and wealth."*

3.) Provide teens with a basic knowledge of God's principles of handling money.

The study is designed to teach and help teens practically apply foundational financial principles from God's Word.

The Primary Responsibilities of the Leader

1.) Unconditionally love and encourage your students.

People are more receptive to spiritual truth when they have been loved. People want to know how much you care before they care how much you know.

2.) Hold your students accountable to complete the assignments.

Be a model of faithfulness. *"Everyone, after he has been fully trained, will be like his teacher"* (Luke 6:40). The leader must be faithful in every area. Always arrive early, pray consistently for your students, know the memory verses fluently, and have your homework and practical exercises prepared.

3.) Conform to the Crown Financial Ministries' procedure of leading the study.

* See note on p. 12.

Information Leaders Need to Know

1.) **The *Discovering God's Way of Handling Money* Teen Study is designed to be taught in a variety of settings: one-on-one, in a small group, in a Sunday school class, and in a Christian school or home school environment.**

This Leader's Guide contains directions for how the Teen Study should be taught in each of these settings.

2.) **How does a leader become qualified to lead the Teen Study?**

Crown Financial Ministries has a training requirement for the leaders of its adult financial study. However, for the Teen Study we only ask you to study the first 10 pages of this Leader's Guide.

3.) **The leader is the key.**

For the Teen Study to be successful, the leader must be prepared. Use illustrations and examples the teens can understand and will find interesting to "bring to life" the Lord's financial principles. The leader should be creative, use humor, and love the students. Make it interesting and fun.

4.) **The Leader's Guide is divided into four sections:**

✓ **Information leaders need to know.** The leaders should study the material on pages 4-10 before leading the class.

✓ **The chapter guides.** There is a guide for each chapter that contains the answers for the questions. The guides are found on pages 11-65.

✓ **How to conduct the study.** This section addresses how the study should be taught in different settings: one-on-one (page 66), in a small group (pages 67-68), in Sunday school (pages 69-70), and in a Christian school or home school (pages 71-72).

✓ **Prayer Logs.** Read more about the Prayer Logs on page 9.

✓ **Student Requirements.** Before each class the students should memorize an assigned Scripture, complete a practical exercise, and answer the assignment questions. Each lesson contains four sets of questions. In the Student Manual, turn to page 10: On this page are question sets 1 and 2. On page 11 you will find question sets 3 and 4.

6.) The classes are designed to meet for approximately 50 minutes. The teacher may elect to modify this time.

7.) Size of the Classes

If you are teaching the Teen Study in a small group setting, we suggest no more than eight students in the group. In a Sunday school or Christian school, there is no class size limitation. However, if there are more than eight students in a class, we recommend that you divide the students into groups of no more than eight. This is possible only if there is one teacher for each group.

Smaller groups allow the teens to be more actively involved and, therefore, more attentive. Larger groups can be intimidating to students who are shy.

8.) What age is this study designed for?

The Teen Study is designed for 13- to 19-year-olds. If you have a group of both younger and older teens, it is suggested that the group be divided according to age. This allows the experience and comprehension level to be similar in each group.

9.) Parental Involvement

Whenever possible, encourage parents to be involved in helping their teens with this study. An excellent resource for parents interested in training their children to be wise money managers is *Financial Parenting* by Larry Burkett. It is available through Crown.

10.) Evangelism

Many people are introduced to Jesus Christ as their Savior when they are young. At the end of Chapter 8 there is a section describing how a person can come to know Christ. Leaders should use this opportunity to share how a person can come to know the Savior.

11.) How to Place an Order

Should you wish to order additional materials, you can contact Crown Financial Ministries in several ways.

✓ **Phone.** Call 1-800-722-1976 any time Monday through Saturday, 24 hours a day.

✓ **Internet.** Visit us at Crown.org and place your order online.

✓ **Mail.** Write us and request a materials catalog at Crown Financial Ministries, PO Box 100, Gainesville GA 30503-0100.

12.) Promoting Financial Products or Services

No one may use their affiliation with Crown Financial Ministries to promote or influence the sale of any investments, financial services, or professional services.

13.) Other Crown Studies

Crown Financial Ministries has studies for four other age categories.

✓ *The ABC's of Handling Money God's Way* for children 7 and younger,

✓ *The Secret of Handling Money God's Way* for ages 8 to 12,

✓ A **Collegiate Study**, and

✓ A variety of **studies for adults**.

14.) More about Crown Financial Ministries

✓ Crown is an interdenominational ministry that trains people to apply biblical financial principles to their lives.

✓ Crown Financial Ministries is a non-profit organization. It is governed by a Board of Directors, none of whom receive a salary from serving the ministry. Crown is a member of the Evangelical Council for Financial Accountability, whose members must adhere to strict standards, including an annual audit.

What to Do Before the First Class

Meet with the students before the first class to begin to love them and communicate the following information.

1.) Review the students' requirements.

The requirements for each chapter are designed to take approximately one hour outside of class. If for any reason someone comes to the class unprepared, they should not be allowed to participate in the discussion. The student requirements are found on page 5 of this Leader's Guide.

2.) Describe the other important "ground rules":

✓ The class opens and closes in prayer.

✓ Scriptures are memorized in the version used in the Crown materials and not in another version of the Bible.

✓ The classes start and stop on time.

✓ No one will be embarrassed by being required to expose his or her financial situation.

✓ Although the class will be fun, nobody should interrupt while the leader or another student is talking.

3.) Dispense the materials.

One Student Manual is required for each student.

4.) Assign the Chapter 1 lesson.

The assignment is found on pages 10-11 of the Student Manual and must be completed before attending the first class. The assignment is to memorize Luke 16:11, answer the questions, and read the Introduction Notes.

Prayer Log

To help the students develop a more consistent prayer life, we use **Prayer Logs**.

✓ In a class that has more than eight students, divide the students into prayer groups of no more than seven or eight people. Then toward the end of each class, ask the students to gather with their group to take prayer requests and share any answers to prayer. Students should stay in the same group during the entire study.

✓ During the first meeting, ask each person to tell the others in their group the information asked for at the top of the Prayer Log—name, phone number, etc.

✓ One Prayer Log should be filled out for each person in a group. The Prayer Logs are located in the back of the Student Manual and the Leader's Guide.

✓ Ask the participants to complete their own entry in the Prayer Log before coming to class to save time. Each member is encouraged to pray daily for everyone in the group during the study.

Examine the sample Prayer Log below.

"Pray for one another" (JAMES 5:16).

Name _Mary Johnson_   Parents _George and Jane_

Home phone _555-9876_   Brothers and Sisters _Tom_

Cell phone _555-7853_   _Alice_

E-mail _mary@provider.com_

Home address _321 Victor Avenue_

Orlando, FL 32750

WEEK	PRAYER REQUEST(S)	ANSWERS TO PRAYER
1	For Tom to get over the flu and for Ann, a neighbor, to come to Christ.	
2	For wisdom on science test and for Ann to come to know the Lord.	Tommy completely well.
3	For a safe family vacation and for Ann to know the Lord.	Science test went well.

Loving the Students

One of the primary responsibilities of the leader is to love the students. Remember, teens want to know how much you care before they care how much you know. The leader needs to grasp every opportunity to love the students both inside and outside of the class.

Love the students outside of class.

1.) **We suggest that the leaders contact each student once or twice during the study to encourage them.**

   The contacts may be by telephone, by mail or e-mail, or in person.

2.) **Consider organizing a social event for the students.**

   This might be a dessert get-together, a picnic, or any other relaxed setting that encourages the development of relationships.

3.) **Consider doing something special as a "graduation" gift when the study is completed. The following are suggestions:**

   ✓ Take a photograph of the class and give it to the students.

   ✓ Present a graduation certificate.

   ✓ Hold a social event to celebrate graduation.

Love the students inside of class.

1.) **The leader's attitude should be humble and caring—not a critical or a "know-it-all" attitude.**

   We are students among students in that we all are growing in understanding the unfathomable Word of God.

2.) **After students answer a question, encourage, affirm, and thank them.**

   ✓ If an answer is incorrect, be careful not to discourage a student by responding harshly or negatively.

   ✓ Maintain good eye contact and be attentive. We communicate much through our body language.

Chapter 1

Introduction

Overview

The primary objectives for this class are to begin to develop close relationships among the participants, to reinforce the study requirements, and to study some of the foundational issues of what the Bible says about money.

NOTE: The blank space following most agenda numbers is for the leader to fill in the scheduled time. For example, if your class begins at 7:00, #2 would read 7:00, #3 would read 7:05, and so forth. This is designed to help the leader monitor the time so the class will end punctually.

Agenda

1.) Open in prayer.

2.) _____ (5 minutes) Have each person recite from memory:

"Therefore if you have not been faithful in the use of worldly* wealth, who will entrust the true riches to you?" (Luke 16:11, *see note on p.12)

3.) _____ (30 minutes) Begin the **Check It Out!** discussion.

Introduction

Memorize It!

"Therefore if you have not been faithful in the use of worldly* wealth, who will entrust the true riches to you?" (Luke 16:11)

* The word "worldly" from the NIV has been substituted for "unrighteous" in the NASB to clarify the meaning.

Check It Out!

NOTE: Crown's comments, enclosed in brackets, will follow most questions. Following Crown's comments will be space for the leader's answers.

1.) Read Isaiah 55:8-9.

Based on this passage, do you think God's principles of handling money are different from the way most people handle money? [God's principles are entirely different than those people use to manage their money.]

What do you think would be the greatest difference(s)? [Most people do not believe the Lord plays a personal role in finances, but Scripture reveals He has the major role.]

2.) How do the following influence the way you spend?

Comparing your spending with that of friends —

Watching TV programs and commercials —

The Internet —

Studying the Bible —

Should your relationship with Christ influence the way you spend money? If so, how?

Do you think the Lord wants you to change the way you spend money? If so, what are some of the things you believe need changing?

3.) Read Luke 16:11.

What does this verse say about handling money and receiving true riches? [How we handle money has a direct impact on our receiving true riches.]

What do you think are the "true riches" referred to in this verse? [The true riches center around knowing the Lord.]

4.) Read the Introductory Notes on pages 12-13.

What information especially interested you?

Why do you think the Bible says so much about money?

Remaining Agenda

1.) _____ (15 minutes) Review what the students are required to do for the next chapter:

✓ Complete the **Check It Out!** questions on pages 16-19. (Note that there are five sets of questions instead of the usual four.)

✓ Memorize 1 Chronicles 29:11-12.

✓ Read the **God's Part & Our Part Notes** on pages 20-26.

✓ Complete the **Put It into Practice!** exercises ("Recording Income and Spending" on page 29 and the "Deed" on page 31).

✓ Complete the **Prayer Logs.** If the class is larger than eight, divide into groups of not more than eight. Each participant shold have one Prayer Log for each person in his or her group, including himself or herself.

2.) _____ (5 minutes) Take prayer requests and note them in the **Prayer Logs**.

3.) End in prayer.

Chapter 2
God's Part & Our Part

Overview

In many respects this is the most important section, because the remainder of the study builds upon understanding God's Part and Our Part. The Lord's ownership of all things and our responsibility to be a faithful steward are the most theological in nature, and the teacher must work hard to keep the students' interest.

Agenda

1.) Open in prayer.

2.) _____ (5 minutes) Have each person recite from memory:

"Everything in the heavens and earth is yours, O Lord, and this is your kingdom. We adore you as being in control of everything. Riches and honor come from you alone, and you are the Ruler of all mankind; your hand controls power and might, and it is at your discretion that men are made great and given strength" (1 Chronicles 29:11-12, TLB).

3.) _____ (5 minutes) Confirm that everyone has started the **Put It into Practice!** exercise "Recording Income and Spending" on page 29 in the Student Manual and has completed the "Deed" on page 31.

4.) _____ (35 minutes) Begin the **Check It Out!** discussion.

God's Part & Our Part

Memorize It!

"Everything in the heavens and earth is yours, O Lord, and this is your kingdom. We adore you as being in control of everything. Riches and honor come from you alone, and you are the Ruler of all mankind; your hand controls power and might, and it is at your discretion that men are made great and given strength" (1 Chronicles 29:11-12, TLB).

Put It into Practice!

- Read the material on pages 26-28.
- Begin recording your income and spending (see page 29).
- Complete the "Deed" on page 31.

Check It Out!

1.) Read Deuteronomy 10:14 and 1 Corinthians 10:26.

What do these verses have to say about your possessions and who owns them? [The Lord owns everything in the world.]

Read the following verses. What do they say God owns?

Leviticus 25:23	[God owns all the land.]
Psalm 50:10-12	[God owns all the animals.]
Haggai 2:8	[God owns all the gold and silver.]

How often do you recognize the true owner of your possessions? Share two practical suggestions that will help you recognize God's ownership of your things.

[**Comment:** Change your vocabulary by dropping the possessive pronouns ("my," "mine," and "ours") and substituting "His" or "the" instead. For 30 days, each morning and night, meditate on and prayerfully recite 1 Chronicles 29:11-12.]

1.)

2.)

2.) Read 1 Chronicles 29:11-12.

What do these verses say about the Lord's ability to control circumstances? [The Lord is in control of all circumstances.]

Do you normally recognize the Lord's control in your life? In the lives of others? If not, how can you become more consistent in recognizing His control?

3.) Read Genesis 45:4-8 and Romans 8:28.

Why is it important to realize that God controls and uses even the difficult times in your life? [God works every circumstance for good in the life of the person who loves Him and is yielded to Him as Lord. Joseph suffered difficulties, but God used them for ultimate good.]

Describe a difficult time you have experienced. How did the Lord use it for good in your life?

Read Psalm 34:9-10 and Matthew 6:31-33. What has the Lord promised about meeting your needs? [God has promised to provide our needs if we seek first the kingdom of God and His righteousness.]

How does this apply to you today? [The Lord continues to provide for us today.]

4.) Read 1 Corinthians 4:2.

According to this verse, what are you required to do as a steward? [We are responsible to be *faithful* as stewards.]

How would you define a steward? [A steward is a manager of another's property.]

Read Luke 16:10. Describe the principle found in this verse. [If a person is unfaithful in a little matter, he or she wil be unfaithful in a large matter.]

How does this apply in your situation?

5.) Read the God's Part & Our Part Notes on pages 20-26.

Write here what interested you most in the Notes.

How will you apply what you have learned?

What benefits do you think you will experience when you do these things?

*Please write your prayer requests in your **Prayer Log** before coming to class.*

Remaining Agenda

1.) _____ (5 minutes) Review what the students are required to do for the next chapter:

   ✓ Complete the **Check It Out!** questions on pages 34-36 in the Student Manual.

   ✓ Memorize Proverbs 22:7.

   ✓ Read the **Debt Notes** on pages 38-41.

   ✓ Complete the **Put It into Practice!** exercise ("Money-Saving Ideas" on pages 42-43) and continue to record income and spending on the worksheet on page 37.

2.) _____ (5 minutes) Take prayer requests and note them in the **Prayer Logs**.

3.) End in prayer.

Chapter 3

Debt

Overview

Debt is a serious struggle for many and is discouraged in Scripture. One of the primary objectives of this session should be to challenge the students to establish the goal of staying debt free.

Agenda

1.) Open in prayer.

2.) _____ (5 minutes) Have each person recite from memory:

"Just as the rich rule the poor, so the borrower is servant to the lender" (Proverbs 22:7, TLB).

3.) _____ (5 minutes) Confirm that everyone has completed the **Put It into Practice!** exercise "Money-Saving Ideas" on pages 42-43 in the Student Manual and is continuing to record income and spending on page 37.

4.) _____ (35 minutes) Begin the **Check It Out!** discussion.

Debt

"Just as the rich rule the poor, so the borrower is servant to the lender" (Proverbs 22:7, TLB).

Put It into Practice!

- Complete the "Money-Saving Ideas" on pages 42-43.
- Continue recording your income and spending on the worksheet on page 37.

Check It Out!

1.) Read Deuteronomy 28:1-2, 12, 15, 43-45.

According to these passages, how was debt viewed in the Old Testament? [Debt was considered a curse. Being free from debt (being a lender) was a blessing.]

What was the cause of someone getting in debt (becoming a borrower) or getting out of debt (becoming a lender)? [Disobedience led to debt and obedience led to getting out of debt (being a lender).]

Read Proverbs 22:7 and Romans 13:8. What does each of these Scriptures say about debt?

Proverbs 22:7	[The person in debt is servant to the lender.]

Romans 13:8	[We are encouraged to stay out of debt.]

2.) Read Psalm 37:21 and Proverbs 3:27-28.

What do these verses say about paying debts?

| *Psalm 37:21* | [A person who borrows but does not repay debts is called "wicked."] |

| *Proverbs 3:27-28* | [Pay debts promptly if you have the resources. Many are taught to delay repayment to use other people's money as long as possible, but this is not biblical.] |

How will you apply what these verses say in your own life?

3.) How would you define cosigning?

[Cosigning is when someone become legally responsible for the debt of another.]

Read Proverbs 17:18 and Proverbs 22:26-27. What does the Bible say about cosigning (some Bible translations refer to this as "striking hands" or "surety")?

| *Proverbs 17:18* | [It is poor judgment to cosign.] |

| *Proverbs 22:26-27* | [Do not cosign. If you do, you may lose your assets.] |

4.) Read the Debt Notes on pages 38-41.

Are you in debt? If so, what steps do you feel the Lord wants you to take to become free of debt?

What did you learn about debt that proved to be especially interesting?

*Please write your prayer requests in your **Prayer Log** before coming to class.*

Remaining Agenda

1.) _____ (5 minutes) Review what the students are required to do for the next chapter:

✓ Complete the **Check It Out!** questions on pages 46-49 in the Student Manual.

✓ Memorize Proverbs 12:15.

✓ Read the **Counsel Notes** on pages 50-53.

✓ Complete the **Put It into Practice!** exercise ("Your Checking Account" on pages 54-57) and continue to record income and spending on the worksheet on page 58.

2.) _____ (5 minutes) Take prayer requests and note them in the **Prayer Logs**.

3.) End in prayer.

Reminder for Leaders: Encourage your students to continue to meditate on 1 Chronicles 29:11-12 to more consistently recognize God's role in their lives.

Chapter 4

Counsel

Overview

Everyone should seek counsel when they need to make major financial decisions. Our culture discourages people from seeking counsel.

Remember to illustrate each major principle with a brief story your students can understand and respond to.

Agenda

1.) Open in prayer.

2.) _____ (5 minutes) Have each person recite from memory:

"The way of a fool is right in his own eyes, but a wise man is he who listens to counsel" (Proverbs 12:15).

3.) _____ (5 minutes) Confirm that everyone has completed the **Put It into Practice!** exercise "Your Checking Account" on pages 54-57 in the Student Manual and is continuing to record income and spending on page 58.

4.) _____ (35 minutes) Begin the **Check It Out!** discussion.

Chapter 4 — Counsel

Memorize It!

"The way of a fool is right in his own eyes, but a wise man is he who listens to counsel" (Proverbs 12:15).

Put It into Practice!

- Complete "Your Checking Account" on pages 54-57.
- Continue recording your income and spending on the worksheet on page 58.

Check It Out!

1.) Read Proverbs 12:15, Proverbs 13:10, and Proverbs 15:22.

What are some of the benefits of seeking counsel?

Proverbs 12:15	[The person who listens to counsel is wise.]

Proverbs 13:10	[Wisdom comes to those who seek counsel but strife to those who don't.]

Proverbs 15:22	[Plans succeed with counsel but fail without it.]

Have you ever asked someone for advice on something? What were the benefits of doing so?

What stops you from seeking counsel?

2.) Read Psalm 16:7 and Psalm 32:8.

Does the Lord counsel us? [The Lord does counsel His people.]

Have you ever suffered because you didn't seek the Lord's counsel? If so, describe what happened.

How do you seek the Lord's counsel? [We seek the counsel of the Lord primarily through prayer, the Bible, and godly people.]

Read Psalm 119:105, 2 Timothy 3:16-17, and Hebrews 4:12. What do each of these verses tell us about the Scriptures?

Psalm 119:105	[The Bible helps guide our path.]
2 Timothy 3:16-17	[God gave us the Scriptures to train and equip us for godly living.]
Hebrews 4:12	[The Word of God is alive and is able to judge our thoughts and intentions.]

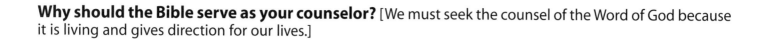

Why should the Bible serve as your counselor? [We must seek the counsel of the Word of God because it is living and gives direction for our lives.]

Do you regularly read and study the Bible? If not, what prevents you?

3.) Read Proverbs 1:8-9.

Who should be among your counselors? [Our parents should be among our counselors.]

Who does Psalm 1:1 say would not be a good counselor? [Avoid wicked counselors.]

Read Proverbs 12:5. Why should you avoid the counsel of these people? [The thoughts of the wicked are not controlled by the Holy Spirit and are deceitful.]

4.) Read the Counsel Notes on pages 50-53.

What in this section particularly interested you?

Do you seek counsel when making a major financial decision? If not, how will you do so in the future?

*Please write your prayer requests in your **Prayer Log** before coming to class.*

Remaining Agenda

1.) _____ (5 minutes) Review what the students are required to do for the next chapter:

✓ Complete the **Check It Out!** questions on pages 60-63 in the Student Manual.

✓ Memorize Leviticus 19:11.

✓ Read the **Honesty Notes** on pages 64-69.

✓ Complete the **Put It into Practice!** exercise ("Estimated Budget" on pages 71-73) and continue to record income and spending on the worksheet on page 70.

2.) _____ (5 minutes) Take prayer requests and note them in the **Prayer Logs**.

3.) End in prayer.

Chapter 5

Honesty

Overview

Dishonest practices are common, but the Lord demands that His people act with total honesty. This section is one of the most challenging of the entire study.

Agenda

1.) Open in prayer.

2.) _____ (5 minutes) Have each person recite from memory:

"You shall not steal, nor deal falsely, nor lie to one another" (Leviticus 19:11).

3.) _____ (5 minutes) Confirm that everyone has completed the **Put It into Practice!** exercise "Estimated Budget" on pages 71-73 in the Student Manual and is continuing to record income and spending on page 70.

4.) _____ (35 minutes) Begin the **Check It Out!** discussion.

Honesty

Memorize It!

"You shall not steal, nor deal falsely, nor lie to one another" (Leviticus 19:11).

Put It into Practice!

- Continue recording your income and spending on the worksheet on page 70.
- Complete the "Estimated Budget" on pages 71-73.

Check It Out!

1.) Read Leviticus 19:11-13, Deuteronomy 25:13-16, and Ephesians 4:25.

What do these verses say about God's demand for honesty?

Leviticus 19:11-13	[The Lord commands us to be honest.]

Deuteronomy 25:13-16	[The Lord demands honesty in our dealings.]

Ephesians 4:25	[We are not to lie to one another.]

Are you honest in even the smallest matters? If not, what will you do to change?

What are two factors that influence us to act dishonestly? [Some of the factors influencing dishonesty include greed, fearing that God will not provide for us, financial difficulties, and peer pressure.]

1.)

2.)

2.) Read Exodus 18:21-22.

Why does the Lord require honesty in leaders? [The Lord requires leaders to be honest because leaders influence those under their authority either for good or evil.]

According to Proverbs 14:2, can you practice dishonesty and still love God? Why or why not? [No, those who practice dishonesty hate the Lord. When a person is dishonest, he believes that God is unable to provide him with exactly what he needs, is incapable of discovering his dishonesty, and is powerless to discipline him. In short, the dishonest person acts as if the Lord does not exist.]

What do Proverbs 26:28 and Romans 13:9-10 have to say about practicing dishonesty and still loving your neighbor? [A dishonest person hates those whom he hurts, but love does no wrong to a neighbor. Because dishonesty always affects people, we cannot love and be dishonest at the same time.]

3.) Read Psalm 15:1-5 and Proverbs 12:22.

List some of the benefits of honesty.

Psalm 15:1-5	[More intimate fellowship with the Lord.]

Proverbs 12:22	[An honest person is a delight to the Lord.]

Read Proverbs 3:32 and Proverbs 21:6. What are some of the curses of dishonesty?

Proverbs 3:32	[A dishonest person is an abomination to the Lord.]

Proverbs 21:6	[Obtaining wealth by lying yields only temporary gains and eventually leads to death.]

Define restitution: [Restitution involves the return of what was dishonestly acquired, plus a penalty.]

What does Exodus 22:1-4 say about restitution? [Restitution was required under the Old Testament law, and Zaccheus (in Luke 19:8) is an example of a person fulfilling this obligation.]

If you have gotten anything dishonestly, what do you need to do? [Ask forgiveness from the Lord, confess your dishonesty to the one who was harmed, and make restitution. Sometimes restitution is a delicate issue. The question of how to fulfill the principle of restitution should be prayerfully answered.]

What is a bribe? [A bribe is something offered in order to influence a person to do something illegal or improper.]

What does Exodus 23:8 say about bribes? [You must never take a bribe, because it will influence your judgment. The person who is not involved with bribes will live, but a leader who takes bribes will be overthrown.]

4.) Read the Honesty Notes on pages 64-69.

How does the example of Abraham in Genesis 14:21-23 challenge you to be honest even in small things? [Abraham made a commitment to the Lord not to take even a thread or a sandal thong. We need to consider making a similar commitment to be honest even in the smallest matters.]

Ask the Lord to show you any areas of dishonesty in your life. Write below at least three things you will do to deal with those areas.

*Please write your prayer requests in your **Prayer Log** before coming to class.*

Remaining Agenda

1.) _____ (5 minutes) Review what the students are required to do for the next chapter:

✓ Complete the **Check It Out!** questions on pages 76-79 in the Student Manual.

✓ Memorize Acts 20:35.

✓ Read the **Giving Notes** on pages 80-84.

✓ Complete the **Put It into Practice!** exercise ("Beginning Your Budget" on page 85).

2.) _____ (5 minutes) Take prayer requests and note them in the **Prayer Logs**.

3.) End in prayer.

Remind your students: When they become adults and start careers and families, we recommend that they enroll in the adult Crown small group financial study. We also encourage them to listen to Crown programs on their local Christian radio stations and to visit Crown's Web site at Crown.org.

Chapter 6
Giving

Overview

Concentrate on communicating the importance of giving with the proper attitude and how this can bring us closer to Christ.

Agenda

1.) Open in prayer.

2.) _____ (5 minutes) Have each person recite from memory:

"Remember the words of the Lord Jesus, that He Himself said, 'It is more blessed to give than to receive'" (Acts 20:35).

3.) _____ (5 minutes) Confirm that everyone has completed the **Put It into Practice!** exercise "Beginning Your Budget" on page 85 in the Student Manual.

4.) _____ (35 minutes) Begin the **Check It Out!** discussion.

Giving

"Remember the words of the Lord Jesus, that He Himself said, 'It is more blessed to give than to receive'" (Acts 20:35).

Put It into Practice!

- Complete "Beginning Your Budget" on page 85.

Check It Out!

1.) Read 1 Corinthians 13:3 and 2 Corinthians 9:7.

What do they say about giving with a proper attitude?

1 Corinthians 13:3	[Giving without love is of no value to the giver.]

2 Corinthians 9:7	[Do not give grudgingly but cheerfully. The proper attitude is crucial.]

How would you describe your attitude about giving?

How is the principle in Acts 20:35 different from the way most people think about giving?
[The Lord tells us it is more blessed to give than to receive. Most people think the reverse is true.]

List the benefits for the giver which are found in the following passages:

Proverbs 11:24-25	[There is a material increase—in the Lord's way—to the giver.]

Matthew 6:20	[We can lay up treasures in heaven to enjoy throughout all eternity.]

Luke 12:34	[The heart of the giver is drawn to Christ as treasures are given to Him. This is the most important blessing for the giver.]

2.) How would you define the tithe? [Ten percent of our income.]

According to Malachi 3:8-10, was the tithe required under Old Testament Law? [Tithes were required under the law, and it was considered robbing God not to give these required gifts.]

Read 2 Corinthians 8:1-5. Answer the following questions:

What was the financial condition of the churches in Macedonia? [The churches of Macedonia experienced difficult circumstances (*"a great ordeal of affliction"* and *"deep poverty"*).]

How would you describe their giving? [They gave generously (*"beyond their ability"*) and cheerfully (*"abundance of joy"*).]

What step in verse 5 did they take that allowed them to give so generously? [They first gave themselves to the Lord, asking Him to direct their giving. In the same way we need to submit ourselves to the Lord when determining how much to give.]

What can you learn from studying their example?

What do Galatians 6:6 and 1 Timothy 5:17-18 tell you about giving to your church and to those who teach the Scriptures?

Galatians 6:6	[Those who are taught the Scriptures should financially support their teachers.]
1 Timothy 5:17-18	[We are to adequately support those who serve as pastors and teachers.]

3.) Read Isaiah 58:6-11 and Galatians 2:9-10.

What does each have to say about giving to the poor?

Isaiah 58:6-11	[When we give to the poor, the Lord will protect us, answer our prayers, and bless us with His joy.]

Galatians 2:9-10	[The disciples had a deep concern for the poor. After Paul's confirmation to minister to the Gentiles, the only counsel the disciples gave him was not to forget the poor.]

Study Matthew 25:35-45. How does Jesus Christ identify with the poor? [Jesus identifies personally with the poor. When we give to the poor, we are giving to Christ Himself. When we do not give to the poor, we are not giving to Christ, and He is left hungry and naked.]

Are you currently giving to the poor? If not, what is hindering you? [Encourage your students to ask the Lord to bring one poor person into each of their lives.]

 4.) Read the Giving Notes on pages 80-84.

Share what you learned about giving that proved especially interesting.

How will this affect your giving?

*Please write your prayer requests in your **Prayer Log** before coming to class.*

Remaining Agenda

1.) _____ (5 minutes) Review what the students are required to do for the next chapter:

✓ Complete the **Check It Out!** questions on pages 88-91 in the Student Manual.

✓ Memorize Colossians 3:23-24.

✓ Read the **Work Notes** on pages 92-98.

✓ Complete the **Put It into Practice!** exercise ("Job Resume" on pages 99-103).

2.) _____ (5 minutes) Take prayer requests and note them in the **Prayer Logs**.

3.) End in prayer.

Chapter 7

Work

Overview

Work can be one of the most fulfilling or frustrating areas of life. Our job satisfaction depends upon our understanding the Lord's perspective of work.

NOTE: Crown has created an outstanding tool to help teens understand what type of work God created them to do. It's called *Career Direct.*® Visit Crown.org to learn more about it.

Agenda

1.) Open in prayer.

2.) _____ (5 minutes) Have each person recite from memory:

"Whatever you do, do your work heartily, as for the Lord rather than for men.... It is the Lord Christ whom you serve" (Colossians 3:23-24).

3.) _____ (5 minutes) Confirm that everyone has completed the **Put It into Practice!** exercise "Job Resume" on pages 99-103 in the Student Manual.

4.) _____ (35 minutes) Begin the **Check It Out!** discussion.

Work

Memorize It!

"Whatever you do, do your work heartily, as for the Lord rather than for men.... It is the Lord Christ whom you serve" (Colossians 3:23-24).

Check It Out!

Put It into Practice!

- Complete the "Job Resume" on pages 99-103.

1.) Read Genesis 39:2-5, Exodus 36:1-2, and Psalm 75:6-7.

What do they tell us about how the Lord is involved in our work?

Genesis 39:2-5	[The Lord is in control of our success.]
Exodus 36:1-2	[The Lord gives us our skills and understanding.]
Psalm 75:6-7	[The Lord controls promotion and demotion.]

Do you think most people recognize that the Lord is so involved in their work? Why?
[No, most people don't recognize that the Lord plays any role in work primarily because He has chosen to be invisible.]

How will understanding God's involvement affect you at work and school? [Our work attitudes and actions should be dramatically different from those who do not recognize God's role in work. We should be humble in any of our accomplishments because God gives us skills, success, and promotion.]

2.) Read Proverbs 6:6-11, Proverbs 18:9 and 2 Thessalonians 3:7-10.

What do they say about working hard?

Proverbs 6:6-11 — [The ant is commended as a hard worker.]

Proverbs 18:9 [A lazy person is condemned.]

2 Thessalonians 3:7-10 [If able people choose not to work, we are not to feed them.]

Do you work hard? If not, describe what steps you will take to improve your work habits.

Read Exodus 34:21. What does this verse say about rest? [Hard work should be balanced with adequate rest and by other biblical priorities. Even during busy times, one day of rest each week was required.]

Do you get sufficient rest? If not, how could you increase your rest time?

3.)

Read Colossians 3:22-25.

For whom do you really work? [We work for the Lord.]

Read 1 Peter 2:18. What does this verse say to you? [We should obey our employer—even one who is not good and gentle.]

How will this understanding change your work habits? [This perspective enables you to make a sincere effort—even in difficult circumstances—to serve your boss with a good attitude.]

Read Matthew 22:17-21 and Romans 13:1-7. According to these verses, does the Lord require us to pay taxes to the government? Why? [Yes, we are required to pay taxes so the government can serve the public.]

4.) Read the Work Notes on pages 92-98.

What did you find especially interesting?

Do you usually recognize that you are working for the Lord? If not, what will you do to improve this?

*Please write your prayer requests in your **Prayer Log** before coming to class.*

Remaining Agenda

1.) _____ (5 minutes) Review what the students are required to do for the next chapter:

✓ Complete the **Check It Out!** questions on pages 106-109 in the Student Manual.

✓ Memorize Proverbs 21:20.

✓ Read the **Saving Notes** on pages 110-115.

✓ Complete the **Put It into Practice!** exercise ("Your Savings Account" on page 116).

2.) _____ (5 minutes) Take prayer requests and note them in the **Prayer Logs**.

3.) End in prayer.

Chapter 8

Saving

Agenda

1.) Open in prayer.

2.) _____ (5 minutes) Have each person recite from memory:

"The wise man saves for the future, but the foolish man spends whatever he gets" (Proverbs 21:20, TLB).

3.) _____ (5 minutes) Confirm that everyone has completed the **Put It into Practice!** exercise "Your Savings Account" on page 116 in the Student Manual.

4.) _____ (35 minutes) Begin the **Check It Out!** discussion.

Chapter 8 — Saving

Memorize It!

"The wise man saves for the future, but the foolish man spends whatever he gets" (Proverbs 21:20, TLB).

Put It into Practice!

- Complete "Your Savings Account" on page 116.

Check It Out!

1.) Read Genesis 41:34-36, Proverbs 21:20, and Proverbs 30:24-25.

What do these passages say to you about saving?

Genesis 41:34-36	[Joseph saved during a time of plenty to prepare for a coming famine.]

Proverbs 21:20	[Those who are wise save, but the foolish only spend.]

Proverbs 30:24-25	[Ants are commended as wise because they save.]

How will you begin to save if you are not yet saving?

2.) Read Proverbs 21:5, Proverbs 24:27, and Proverbs 27:23-24.

Identify investment principles and share how you can apply them.

Proverbs 21:5	[Be a diligent, steady plodder and not a hasty investor.]
Proverbs 24:27	[Begin your career before buying a house.]
Proverbs 27:23-24	[Be aware of what is happening to your investments.]

3.) How would you define gambling?

[Gambling is defined as playing games of chance for money, betting, and taking great risks.]

What are some of the common forms of gambling? [Some of today's more common forms of gambling are casino wagering, betting on sporting events, horse races, dog races, and state-run lotteries.]

Why do you think people gamble? [Most people are motivated to gamble by greed, the desire to get rich quick, and by the prospect of getting something for nothing. Many want to become wealthy so they can quit working.]

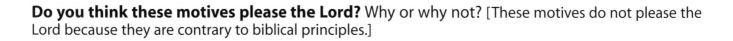

Do you think these motives please the Lord? Why or why not? [These motives do not please the Lord because they are contrary to biblical principles.]

Read Proverbs 28:20 and Proverbs 28:22. According to these passages, why do you think a godly person should not gamble? [A person who hastens after wealth is identified as evil and will experience poverty. Please encourage your students never to bet even one penny. State lotteries are particularly enticing—they have been legalized by the government, they are glamorized by the media, and the jackpots are often so large they are difficult to ignore.]

How does gambling violate the scriptural principles of working hard and being a faithful steward of the Lord's possessions? [Gambling is contrary to the scriptural principles of diligent work and faithful stewardship. No productive work is required in gambling; thus, a person's character is not properly developed. The odds of winning are absurdly low, and a gambler is wasting the possessions the Lord has entrusted to him.]

4.) Read the Saving Notes on pages 110-115.

What proved especially helpful?

Study the principle of compound interest on pages 111-112. Assume you earned 10 percent and saved $20.00 each week (about $1,000 per year). Approximately how much would you accumulate by age 65 if you started saving today? $ _____ (For answer, refer to the graph on page 112.)

*Please write your prayer requests in your **Prayer Log** before coming to class.*

Remaining Agenda

1.) _____ (5 minutes) Review what the students are required to do for the next chapter:

✓ Complete the **Check It Out!** questions on pages 118-121 in the Student Manual.

✓ Memorize 1 Timothy 4:12.

✓ Read the **Friends Notes** on pages 122-126.

✓ Complete the **Put It into Practice!** exercise ("Your Financial Goals" on pages 127-129).

2.) _____ (5 minutes) Take prayer requests and note them in the **Prayer Logs**.

3.) End in prayer.

Chapter 9

Friends

Overview

In this class we explore a number of practical issues that teens should understand: selecting friends, partiality, and taking care of themselves physically.

Agenda

1.) Open in prayer.

2.) _____ (5 minutes) Have each person recite from memory:

"Let no one look down on your youthfulness, but rather in speech, conduct, love, faith and purity, show yourself an example of those who believe" (1 Timothy 4:12).

3.) _____ (5 minutes) Confirm that everyone has completed the **Put It into Practice!** exercise ("Your Financial Goals" on pages 127-129 in the Student Manual) and is budgeting faithfully.

4.) _____ (35 minutes) Begin the **Check It Out!** discussion.

Friends

Memorize It!

"Let no one look down on your youthfulness, but rather in speech, conduct, love, faith and purity, show yourself an example of those who believe" (1 Timothy 4:12).

Put It into Practice!

- Complete "Your Financial Goals" on pages 127-129.

Check It Out!

1.) According to 1 Corinthians 15:33, do our friends influence us?

Why is it important to have a godly group of friends? [Our friends have a massive influence on us—either for good or bad.]

Read 1 Timothy 4:12. What does this verse say about how young people should be an example? [In all areas of life, young people should model godly living.]

Describe some ways you can be an example and influence others to handle money in a way that will please the Lord.

Define partiality: [Favoring one person over another.]

2.) Read Leviticus 19:15, Deuteronomy 10:17 and James 2:1-9.

What does Scripture say about partiality (showing favoritism)?

Leviticus 19:15	[Do not be partial to the poor or to the great.]

Deuteronomy 10:17	[The Lord is not partial.]

James 2:1-9	[Do not show favoritism to the wealthy. It is a sin to be partial.]

Do you tend to favor the friendship of those who are rich or popular over others? Why or why not?

If you believe you are partial, read Romans 12:16 and Philippians 2:3. What guidance do these verses give you to overcome partiality?

Romans 12:16	[Be of the same mind toward each other.]

Philippians 2:3	[Consider other people as more important than yourself.]

3.) Read 1 Corinthians 3:16-17.

If you have invited Jesus Christ into your life, where does God dwell? [He lives in you.]

Since your body is a temple that God lives in, how should you care for yourself physically?
[We should try to keep our bodies in good physical condition by eating properly and getting adequate exercise and sleep.]

Do you eat nutritious food and get enough exercise and sleep? If not, why?

4.) Read the Friends Notes on pages 122-126.

What did you find most interesting in this section?

How will what you learned impact your life?

*Please write your prayer requests in your **Prayer Log** before coming to class.*

Remaining Agenda

1.) _____ (5 minutes) Review what the students are required to do for the next chapter:

✓ Complete the **Check It Out!** questions on pages 132-135 in the Student Manual.

✓ Memorize Philippians 4:11-13.

✓ Read the **Go For It! Notes** on pages 136-140.

✓ Complete the **Put It into Practice!** exercises ("Insurance Needs" on page 141 and "Your Financial Statement" on pages 142-144).

2.) _____ (5 minutes) Take prayer requests and note them in the **Prayer Logs**.

3.) End in prayer.

Chapter 10
Go For It!

Overview

This class concentrates on determining our God-given standard of living. In some respects this section is a summary of the entire study.

Agenda

1.) Open in prayer.

2.) _____ (5 minutes) Have each person recite from memory:

"I have learned to be content in whatever circumstances I am. I know how to get along with humble means, and I also know how to live in prosperity. . . . I can do all things through Him who strengthens me" (Philippians 4:11-13).

3.) _____ (5 minutes) Confirm that everyone has completed the **Put It into Practice!** exercises ("Insurance Needs" on page 141 and "Your Financial Statement" on pages 142-144 in the Student Manual) and is budgeting faithfully.

4.) _____ (35 minutes) Begin the **Check It Out!** discussion.

Go For It!

Memorize It!

"I have learned to be content in whatever circumstances I am. I know how to get along with humble means, and I also know how to live in prosperity.…I can do all things through Him who strengthens me" (Philippians 4:11-13).

Put It into Practice!

- Complete "Insurance Needs" on page 141.
- Complete "Your Financial Statement" on pages 142-144.

Check It Out!

1.) How would you define contentment? [Contentment is an inner peace that accepts what God has chosen for us in our current circumstances.]

What do Philippians 4:11-13, 1 Timothy 6:6-8, and Hebrews 13:5-6 have to say about contentment?

Philippians 4:11-13	[Contentment is not something that occurs naturally. It is learned. We can learn to be content in any circumstance.]
1 Timothy 6:6-8	[Godliness with contentment is great gain. We cannot take anything with us when we die, and we should be content with having our basic needs satisfied.]
Hebrews 13:5-6	[Because the Lord is our Protector and Provider, we can be content. We are admonished not to love money and to be content with what we have.]

How does our culture discourage contentment?

2.) Complete the Insurance Needs exercise on page 141.

Look up the word "prosperity" in the dictionary. What does it mean?

3.) Read Joshua 1:8 and Hebrews 11:36-40.

What do these passages say to you about financial prosperity for the believer?

Joshua 1:8	[Knowing and obeying all of the commands in the Scriptures forms the foundation for prosperity.]

Hebrews 11:36-40	[Even godly people exercising faith have experienced poverty and difficult circumstances.]

Think about the lives of Job, Joseph, King David, and Paul. Check out their stories in the Bible. Describe how they experienced times of plenty and times when there wasn't a lot of money. [Job, Joseph, David, and Paul each experienced periods of plenty and times of want.]

Is financial prosperity something all Christians should always experience? Why or why not? [Once a person has fulfilled all areas of being a faithful steward, he or she is in a position for the Lord to prosper them financially. However, the Lord may not prosper us for one of three reasons: 1) He is building our character (Romans 5:3-4); 2) He needs to discipline us in areas of our lives where there is sin (Hebrews 12:6, 10); or 3) God is exercising His sovereignty (Hebrews 11:36-40).]

Describe the lifestyle you would like to have when you grow up (what kind of home, transportation, clothes, giving, vacations, etc.).

Estimate how much these will cost each month and how much you'll need to earn.

How do you plan on accomplishing this?

4.) Read the Go for It! Notes on pages 136-140.

What concept interested you most in the Notes?

Describe any spending habits you sense the Lord wants you to change.

Thinking of the entire study, what was the most helpful part for you?

*Please write your prayer requests in your **Prayer Log** before coming to class.*

Remaining Agenda

1.) _____ (10 minutes) Take "long-term" prayer requests and note them on the **Prayer Logs**.

2.) End in prayer.

Reminder to Leaders: We suggest that you write your students personal, encouraging letters summarizing what you appreciate most about them. May the Lord richly bless you in every way for your role in equipping these young people to handle money from a biblical perspective.

How to . . . One-on-One

1.) Before beginning the study the leader should:

✓ Review pages 4-10 of this Leader's Guide.

✓ Meet with the student to review the course requirements.

2.) Before each class the leader should:

✓ Review the material for that chapter in the Leader's Guide.

✓ Memorize the assigned Scripture.

✓ Answer the **Check It Out!** questions in the Leader's Guide.

✓ Remember to pray daily for your student.

3.) How to conduct the class:

Each of the 10 lessons is conducted in the same way. Turn in the Leader's Guide to the appropriate chapter and follow the agenda. Use this procedure when teaching one-on-one:

✓ Open with prayer.

✓ Recite the **Memorize It!** Scripture.

✓ Confirm that the **Put It into Practice!** exercise has been completed.

✓ Conduct the **Check It Out!** discussion, proceeding as follows:

■ Read the Scriptures for set 1 of the questions.

■ Ask the student to answer the questions for that set.

■ The leader should then answer the questions for that set. After answering the questions the leader should then initiate dialogue to make certain the student understands the issue under discussion.

■ Repeat this procedure for each of the four sets (five sets in Chapter 5).

✓ Complete the items listed in the Remaining Agenda in consecutive order.

✓ Share prayer requests and write them in the **Prayer Logs**.

✓ End in prayer.

How to . . . Small Group

1.) Before starting the study the leader should:

✓ Review pages 4-10 of this Leader's Guide.

✓ Meet with the students to review the course requirements.

2.) Before each class the leader should:

✓ Review the material for that chapter in the Leader's Guide.

✓ Memorize the assigned Scripture.

✓ Answer the **Check It Out!** questions in the Leader's Guide.

✓ Remember to pray daily for your students.

3.) How to conduct the class

Each of the 10 classes is conducted in the same way. Turn in the Leader's Guide to the appropriate chapter and follow the agenda. Use this procedure when teaching a small group:

✓ Open with prayer.

✓ The students individually recite the **Memorize It!** Scripture.

✓ Confirm that students have completed the **Put It into Practice!** exercise.

✓ Conduct the **Check It Out!** group discussion, proceeding as follows:

■ Assign different students to read the Scriptures for set 1 of the questions.

■ Proceed in a circle asking every person to answer all the questions for that set.

■ The leader should then answer the questions for that set. After answering the questions the leader should then initiate dialogue to make certain the students understand the principle under discussion.

■ Repeat this procedure for each of the four sets (five sets in Chapter 5).

✓ Complete the items listed in the Remaining Agenda in consecutive order.

✓ Share prayer requests and write them in the **Prayer Logs**.

✓ End in prayer.

Classroom Dynamics

The most effective group discussions involve group interaction and member-to-member participation.

In Diagram 1 the sole focus is on the teacher, who does all the talking. The students are passive. This is not how the Teen Study is designed to be taught.

Diagram 2 reflects the people in a group interacting with one another, and a leader who guides and facilitates the discussion. The leader must establish an environment in which students have the freedom to express their insights and questions.

Diagram 1 – Incorrect Method   *Diagram 2 – Correct Method*

   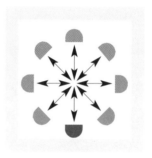

LEADER   LEADER

How to . . . Sunday School

1.) Before beginning the study the teacher should:

✓ Review pages 4-10 of this Leader's Guide.

✓ Meet with students to review the course requirements.

2.) Before each class the teacher should:

✓ Review the material for that lesson in the Leader's Guide.

✓ Memorize the assigned Scripture.

✓ Answer the **Check It Out!** questions in the Leader's Guide.

✓ Pray daily for your students.

3.) If possible, divide into groups of seven or eight.

If the class has more than eight students, we recommend that you divide into smaller groups of no more than eight students. This will be possible only if you have a teacher for each group. Smaller groups allow the teens to be more actively involved and more attentive.

4.) How to conduct the class

Each of the 10 lessons is conducted in the same way. Turn in the Leader's Guide to the appropriate chapter and follow the agenda. Use this procedure when teaching in a Sunday school:

✓ Open with prayer.

✓ The students recite the weekly **Memorize It!** Scripture. This can be done by each student in front of the entire class or by the entire class in unison—depending upon the size of the class.

✓ Conduct the group discussion. The discussion should proceed as follows:

■ Assign teens to read the Scriptures for set 1 of the questions.

■ Ask four or five students to answer all the questions for that set.

■ The teacher should then answer the questions for that set. After answering the questions, the teacher should initiate further dialogue to make certain the students understand the issues under discussion.

■ Repeat this procedure for each of the four sets (five sets in Chapter 5).

✓ Complete the items listed in the Remaining Agenda in consecutive order.

✓ Break up into prayer groups of four to eight people, share prayer requests and write them in the **Prayer Logs**.

✓ End in prayer.

Classroom Dynamics

The most effective group discussions involve group interaction and member-to-member participation.

In Diagram 1 the sole focus is on the teacher, who does all the talking. The students are passive. This is not how the Teen Study is designed to be taught.

Diagram 2 reflects the people in a group interacting with one another, and a leader who guides and facilitates the discussion. The leader must establish an environment in which students have the freedom to express their insights and questions.

Diagram 1 – Incorrect Method   *Diagram 2 – Correct Method*

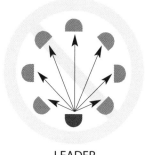   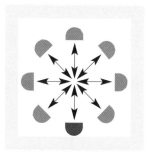

LEADER   LEADER

How to . . . School

1.) What the teacher should know:

This study is designed for both Christian and home schools.

On the following pages are 10 examinations you can use. Each chapter has one test with the answers for the teacher and one test without the answers for the students. Please photocopy as many of the student examinations as you need.

Should you choose to develop your own examination, you may use any of the questions contained on the enclosed tests.

There are four sets of questions in each chapter. If you conduct this study five days a week, the students can complete the questions in class for four days. The fifth day can be used for the examination. If you conduct this study one day a week, the students may complete the questions outside of class.

2.) Before beginning the study the teacher should:

✓ Review pages 4-10 of this Leader's Guide.

✓ Meet with students to review the course requirements.

3.) If possible, divide into groups of seven or eight.

If the class has more than eight students, we recommend that you divide into smaller groups of no more than eight students. This will be possible only if you have a teacher for each group. Smaller groups allow the teens to be more actively involved and more attentive.

4.) Before each lesson the teacher should:

✓ Review the material for that chapter in the Leader's Guide.

✓ Memorize the assigned Scripture.

✓ Answer the **Check It Out!** questions in the Leader's Guide.

✓ Pray daily for your students.

5.) How to conduct the class

Each of the 10 lessons is conducted in the same way. Turn in the Leader's Guide to the appropriate chapter and follow the agenda. Use this procedure when teaching in a school:

- ✓ Open with prayer.

- ✓ The students recite the **Memorize It!** Scripture. This can be done by each student in front of the entire class or by the entire class in unison.

- ✓ Conduct the group discussion. The discussion should proceed as follows:

  - ■ Assign teens to read the Scriptures for set 1 of the questions.

  - ■ Ask four or five students to answer all the questions for that set.

  - ■ The teacher should then answer the questions for set 1. After answering the questions, the teacher should initiate further dialogue to make certain the students understand the issues under discussion.

  - ■ Repeat this procedure for each of the four sets (five sets in Chapter 5).

- ✓ Complete the items listed in the Remaining Agenda in consecutive order.

- ✓ Break up into prayer groups of four to eight people, share prayer requests, and write them in the **Prayer Logs**.

- ✓ End in prayer.

Classroom Dynamics

The most effective group discussions involve group interaction and member-to-member participation.

In Diagram 1 the sole focus is on the teacher, who does all the talking. The students are passive. This is not how the Crown Teen Study is designed to be taught.

Diagram 2 reflects the people in a class interacting with one another, and a leader who guides and facilitates the discussion. The teacher must establish an environment in which students have the freedom to express their insights and questions.

Diagram 1 – Incorrect Method

LEADER

Diagram 2 – Correct Method

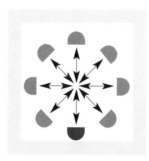

LEADER

Introduction Examination
Chapter 1 – Teacher's Edition

1. Write this chapter's **Memorize It!** Scripture, Luke 16:11. *"Therefore if you have not been faithful in the use of worldly wealth, who will entrust the true riches to you?"*

2. God's economy operates on different principles than those used by most people.

   ❏ **True**   ❏ False

3. What is the most significant difference between the way most people handle money and God's financial principles? **The most striking difference is the living God. Most people think that God is not a factor when it comes to money. Yet according to Scripture, He plays the dominant role.**

4. Can a person who does not yet know the Lord understand God's economy? Why? **No. First Corinthians 2:14 tells us, *"But a natural man does not accept the things of the Spirit of God; for they are foolishness to Him, and he cannot understand them, because they are spiritually appraised."***

5. There is a division of responsibilities in the handling of money. Identify the parties responsible. **God and each of us.**

6. Write an essay on why the Bible says so much about money and possessions.

Introduction Examination

Chapter 1

1. Write this chapter's **Memorize It!** Scripture, Luke 16:11.

2. God's economy operates on different principles than those used by most people.

   ❏ True   ❏ False

3. What is the most significant difference between the way most people handle money and God's financial principles?

4. Can a person who does not yet know the Lord understand God's economy? Why?

5. There is a division of responsibilities in the handling of money. Identify the parties responsible.

6. Write an essay on why the Bible says so much about money and possessions.

God's Part & Our Part Examination
Chapter 2 – Teacher's Edition

1. Write this chapter's **Memorize It!** Scripture, 1 Chronicles 29:11-12. *"Everything in the heavens and earth is yours, O Lord, and this is your kingdom. We adore you as being in control of everything. Riches and honor come from you alone, and you are the Ruler of all mankind; your hand controls power and might, and it is at your discretion that men are made great and given strength."*

2. God is the owner of all your possessions.

   ❏ **True**   ❏ False

3. Circle the three things the Bible identifies as owned by God: **land**, rubies, **gold**, mountains, **cattle**, pizza, The Washington Redskins.

4. God will test some people by asking them to be willing to give up an important possession.

   ❏ **True**   ❏ False

   Give an example of this in the Bible. **Abraham giving up his son Isaac.**

5. The Lord is in control of all circumstances.

   ❏ **True**   ❏ False

6. Give an example of a godly person in Scripture who experienced difficult circumstances while living a righteous life. **Joseph, Daniel, David, and Paul, to name a few.**

7. The name that best describes Our Part in the area of money is: owner, **steward**, shepherd, captain, master.

8. How would you define the name that best describes Our Part? **A steward is a manager or overseer of someone else's property.**

9. Write an essay on God's ownership of your possessions and His control of circumstances. Describe how understanding this will help you learn to be content.

God's Part & Our Part Examination

1. Write this chapter's **Memorize It!** Scripture, 1 Chronicles 29:11-12.

2. God is the owner of all your possessions.
   ❏ True   ❏ False

3. Circle the three things the Bible identifies as owned by God: land, rubies, gold, mountains, cattle, pizza, The Washington Redskins.

4. God will test some people by asking them to be willing to give up an important possession.
   ❏ True   ❏ False

   Give an example of this in the Bible.

5. The Lord is in control of all circumstances.
   ❏ True   ❏ False

6. Give an example of a godly person in Scripture who experienced difficult circumstances while living a righteous life.

7. The name that best describes Our Part in the area of money is: owner, steward, shepherd, captain, master.

8. How would you define the name that best describes Our Part?

9. Write an essay on God's ownership of your possessions and His control of circumstances. Describe how understanding this will help you learn to be content.

Debt Examination
Chapter 3 – Teacher's Edition

1. Write this chapter's **Memorize It!** Scripture, Proverbs 22:7. ***"Just as the rich rule the poor, so the borrower is servant to the lender."***

2. Define debt: **Money that one person is obligated to pay to another.**

3. Which statement best describes the biblical perspective of debt?

   Debt is strongly encouraged.

   <u>Debt is discouraged and is considered unwise.</u>

   Debt in our modern culture is acceptable.

4. Explain the reasons that credit-card companies want you to become a borrower. **Credit-card companies encourage the use of credit cards because of the high interest they earn from borrowers.**

5. Read Deuteronomy 28:1-2, 12 and Deuteronomy 28:15, 43-45. In the Old Testament how was debt viewed? What caused a person to get into debt? **Debt was viewed as a curse that was the result of disobedience.**

6. Define bankruptcy. Describe what the Bible says about bankruptcy. **Bankruptcy is when a court of law declares a person unable to pay his debts. It is discouraged in the Bible.**

7. Define cosigning. Describe God's perspective of cosigning. **Cosigning is the act of becoming legally responsible for the debt of another. Cosigning is discouraged.**

8. Write an essay on why you feel it will be important for you to follow God's perspective of debt. Include any spending choices that you think you may need to make to stay debt-free.

Debt Examination

Chapter 3

1. Write this chapter's **Memorize It!** Scripture, Proverbs 22:7.

2. Define debt:

3. Which statement best describes the biblical perspective of debt?

   Debt is strongly encouraged.

   Debt is discouraged and is considered unwise.

   Debt in our modern culture is acceptable.

4. Explain the reasons that credit-card companies want you to become a borrower.

5. Read Deuteronomy 28:1-2, 12 and Deuteronomy 28:15, 43-45. In the Old Testament how was debt viewed? What caused a person to get into debt?

6. Define bankruptcy. Describe what the Bible says about bankruptcy.

7. Define cosigning. Describe God's perspective of cosigning.

8. Write an essay on why you feel it will be important for you to follow God's perspective of debt. Include any spending choices that you think you may need to make to stay debt-free.

Counsel Examination

Chapter 4 – Teacher's Edition

1. Write this chapter's **Memorize It!** Scripture, Proverbs 12:15. *"The way of a fool is right in his own eyes, but a wise man is he who listens to counsel."*

2. Define counsel: **Seeking the advice of another.**

3. Seeking counsel relieves you of the responsibility to make a decision.

   ❏ True   ❏ **False**

4. Explain the reason for seeking counsel. **We seek counsel to secure suggestions that can help us make good decisions.**

5. Why should the Bible be a source of counsel? **The Word of God is living and active; it contains God's revealed will and provides many principles that are applicable to life.**

6. Which of the following should not be among our counselors? Parents, **wicked people**, pastors, experienced people, **a fortune teller**.

7. How do you seek the counsel of the Lord? **Primarily through a study of His Word and seeking Him in prayer.**

8. Write an essay on what most people think about seeking counsel. How does this contrast with the biblical view of counsel? Include a discussion of how you are going to seek counsel.

Counsel Examination
Chapter 4

1. Write this chapter's **Memorize It!** Scripture, Proverbs 12:15.

2. Define counsel:

3. Seeking counsel relieves you of the responsibility to make a decision.
   ❏ True   ❏ False

4. Explain the reason for seeking counsel.

5. Why should the Bible be a source of counsel?

6. Which of the following should not be among our counselors? Parents, wicked people, pastors, experienced people, a fortune teller.

7. How do you seek the counsel of the Lord?

8. Write an essay on what most people think about seeking counsel. How does this contrast with the biblical view of counsel? Include a discussion of how you are going to seek counsel.

Honesty Examination

1. Write this chapter's **Memorize It!** Scripture, Leviticus 19:11. ***"You shall not steal, nor deal falsely, nor lie to one another."***

2. Answer the following:

We cannot practice dishonesty and love God.	❑ **True**	❑ False
Dishonesty does not always hurt people.	❑ True	❑ **False**
Dishonesty harms efforts of evangelism.	❑ **True**	❑ False
Little lies are not sinful.	❑ True	❑ **False**
Honesty helps confirm God's direction.	❑ **True**	❑ False

3. How would you describe a "healthy" fear of the Lord? How would this healthy fear help you to be honest? **God is a loving Father who, out of infinite love, disciplines His children for their benefit (Hebrews 12:10). A healthy fear of God recognizes that He will discipline us for dishonesty—and this helps us stay honest.**

4. Why is it especially important for leaders to be absolutely honest? **Because they influence those they lead.**

5. Define a bribe. Describe the biblical position on bribes. **A bribe is anything given to a person to influence him or her to do something illegal, wrong, or something that would not normally be done. The taking of bribes is prohibited in Scripture.**

6. Define restitution. How should we apply the principle of restitution? **Restitution is the return of property that was acquired dishonestly. If we have acquired anything dishonestly, we need to return it to its rightful owner. As an expression of repentance, it may require returning more than was originally taken.**

7. Write an essay on why the Lord demands honesty. In the essay answer these questions: Am I consistently honest in even the smallest details? If not, what am I going to do to become an honest person?

Honesty Examination

Chapter 5

1. Write this chapter's **Memorize It!** Scripture, Leviticus 19:11.

2. Answer the following:

We cannot practice dishonesty and love God.	❏ True	❏ False
Dishonesty does not always hurt people.	❏ True	❏ False
Dishonesty harms efforts of evangelism.	❏ True	❏ False
Little lies are not sinful.	❏ True	❏ False
Honesty helps confirm God's direction.	❏ True	❏ False

3. How would you describe a "healthy" fear of the Lord? How would this healthy fear help you to be honest?

4. Why is it especially important for leaders to be absolutely honest?

5. Define a bribe. Describe the biblical position on bribes.

6. Define restitution. How should we apply the principle of restitution?

7. Write an essay on why the Lord demands honesty. In the essay answer these questions: Am I consistently honest in even the smallest details? If not, what am I going to do to become an honest person?

Giving Examination

1. Write this chapter's **Memorize It!** Scripture, Acts 20:35, in its entirety: ***"Remember the words of the Lord Jesus, that He Himself said, 'It is more blessed to give than to receive.'"***

2. Attitudes are important in giving. Describe God's attitude in giving and what our attitude should be. **God's attitude is best expressed in John 3:16: Because He loved, He gave. Our attitude should model His—being a loving giver. We should also be cheerful givers.**

3. How can a person consistently develop the proper attitude in giving? **We need to view everything we give as given to Christ. Then we can consistently give out of a heart of love and gratitude for all He has done for us.**

4. According to Acts 20:35 it is more blessed to give than to receive. Of the following, select three ways a person is blessed:

   Growing closer to God

   Becoming very rich

   Becoming more like Christ

   Laying up treasures in heaven

   Becoming popular among people

5. Read 2 Corinthians 9:6-11. According to this passage, why does the Lord bless us financially when we give? **He provides so that we can meet our needs and so we will have more to give.**

6. Define a tithe. **A tithe is 10 percent of our income.**

7. Write an essay on what the Bible says about giving to the poor. Look up Matthew 25:35-45, Galatians 2:10, Isaiah 58:6-9, Proverbs 21:13, and Proverbs 28:27. Include a discussion of each of these passages in the essay.

Giving Examination
Chapter 6

1. Write this chapter's **Memorize It!** Scripture, Acts 20:35, in its entirety:

2. Attitudes are important in giving. Describe God's attitude in giving and what our attitude should be.

3. How can a person consistently develop the proper attitude in giving?

4. According to Acts 20:35 it is more blessed to give than to receive. Of the following, select three ways a person is blessed:

    Growing closer to God

    Becoming very rich

    Becoming more like Christ

    Laying up treasures in heaven

    Becoming popular among people

5. Read 2 Corinthians 9:6-11. According to this passage, why does the Lord bless us financially when we give?

6. Define a tithe.

7. Write an essay on what the Bible says about giving to the poor. Look up Matthew 25:35-45, Galatians 2:10, Isaiah 58:6-9, Proverbs 21:13, and Proverbs 28:27. Include a discussion of each of these passages in the essay.

Work Examination
Chapter 7 – Teacher's Edition

1. Write this chapter's **Memorize It!** Scripture, Colossians 3:23-24. *"Whatever you do, do your work heartily, as for the Lord rather than for men. . . . It is the Lord Christ whom you serve."*

2. Match the worker to the job:

   Amos   Government worker **(Daniel)**

   David   Doctor **(Luke)**

   Daniel   Seller of purple fabrics **(Lydia)**

   Luke   Fig picker **(Amos)**

   Lydia   Tentmaker **(Paul)**

   Paul   Shepherd and king **(David)**

3. What does the Bible say about hard work and laziness? **Scripture encourages hard work and condemns laziness.**

4. What is the biblical view of rest? **The Old Testament required rest one day out of seven. This is a wise principle for us to follow even today.**

5. Read Daniel 6:1-21. Identify three of the six characteristics of a godly employee as modeled in the life of Daniel. **(1) Honesty (2) Faithfulness (3) Prayerfulness (4) Honors his or her boss (5) Honors fellow employees (6) Shares faith in the Lord with others.**

6. Contrast retirement as it is practiced in our culture with what the Scriptures teach. **Our culture encourages people to retire. The Bible does not.**

7. Define a procrastinator. Is procrastination biblical? **Putting off something that needs to be done now. It is not biblical.**

8. Write an essay on the part that God plays in our work. Include a discussion of how this should affect you at work and school.

Work Examination
Chapter 7

1. Write this chapter's **Memorize It!** Scripture, Colossians 3:23-24.

2. Match the worker to the job:

    Amos   Government worker

    David   Doctor

    Daniel   Seller of purple fabrics

    Luke   Fig picker

    Lydia   Tentmaker

    Paul   Shepherd and king

3. What does the Bible say about hard work and laziness?

4. What is the biblical view of rest?

5. Read Daniel 6:1-21. Identify three of the six characteristics of a godly employee as modeled in the life of Daniel.

6. Contrast retirement as it is practiced in our culture with what the Scriptures teach.

7. Define a procrastinator. Is procrastination biblical?

8. Write an essay on the part that God plays in our work. Include a discussion of how this should affect you at work and school.

Saving Examination
Chapter 8 – Teacher's Edition

1. Write this chapter's **Memorize It!** Scripture, Proverbs 21:20. ***"The wise man saves for the future, but the foolish man spends whatever he gets."***

2. What does the Bible say about saving? How are you going to apply this principle? **The Word of God encourages saving.**

3. There are three factors in compound interest. Circle them:

   Time

   The bank

   Amount

   The stock market

   Interest rate

4. Read the following verses and identify one investment principle from each:

   Proverbs 24:27 — **Build your means of producing an income before you build your home.**

   Proverbs 27:23-24 — **Be aware of the status of your budget and possessions.**

5. What is the biblical view of gambling? **Gambling is discouraged, because it does not develop character or enable a person to benefit from hard work.**

6. Why should adults have a will? **An organized estate is a blessing to the surviving family members. It also enables you to direct how you want to distribute your assets.**

7. Write an essay describing how a person can enter into a relationship with the Lord.

Saving Examination

Chapter 8

1. Write this chapter's **Memorize It!** Scripture, Proverbs 21:20.

2. What does the Bible say about saving? How are you going to apply this principle?

3. There are three factors in compound interest. Circle them:

   Time

   The bank

   Amount

   The stock market

   Interest rate

4. Read the following verses and identify one investment principle from each:

   Proverbs 24:27 —

   Proverbs 27:23-24 —

5. What is the biblical view of gambling?

6. Why should adults have a will?

7. Write an essay describing how a person can enter into a relationship with the Lord.

Friends Examination

1. Write this chapter's **Memorize It!** Scripture, 1 Timothy 4:12. *"Let no one look down on your youthfulness, but rather in speech, conduct, love, faith and purity, show yourself an example to those who believe."*

2. Why is it important to have a group of friends who are godly? **Because we are deeply influenced by our friends and peers.**

3. Describe three ways you can influence others to handle money in a way that will please the Lord.

4. What does the Bible say about paying taxes? **The Scriptures require us to pay the taxes that we owe to help fund the government.**

5. Study 1 Corinthians 3:16-17. According to this passage, why is it important to care for yourself physically? **The Lord lives in our bodies and we should take care of them and keep them in good condition, because they are God's temples.**

6. Write an essay on partiality. Define partiality, discuss the problem, and describe God's perspective of partiality. Include your own struggle with partiality, and how you propose to overcome it.

Friends Examination
Chapter 9

1. Write this chapter's **Memorize It!** Scripture, 1 Timothy 4:12.

2. Why is it important to have a group of friends who are godly?

3. Describe three ways you can influence others to handle money in a way that will please the Lord.

4. What does the Bible say about paying taxes?

5. Study 1 Corinthians 3:16-17. According to this passage, why is it important to care for yourself physically?

6. Write an essay on partiality. Define partiality, discuss the problem, and describe God's perspective of partiality. Include your own struggle with partiality, and how you propose to overcome it.

Go For It! Examination

1. Write this chapter's **Memorize It!** Scripture, Philippians 4:11-13. ***"I have learned to be content in whatever circumstances I am. I know how to get along with humble means, and I also know how to live in prosperity. . . . I can do all things through Him who strengthens me."***

2. Define contentment. **Contentment is an inner peace that accepts what God has chosen for us in our current work, school, and finances.**

3. Describe how a person can learn to be content. **Know what God wants you to do; do what God wants you to do; and trust God to do His part.**

4. Why should godly people not worry or be envious of the wicked who become prosperous? **God tells us that some of the wicked will prosper. However, we are cautioned not to be envious because they will spend an eternity separated from God.**

5. Read Joshua 1:8. According to this passage, what must you do to put yourself in a position to experience prosperity? **You must regularly meditate on the Scriptures and live by everything that is written in them.**

6. If you are faithful to do all that is required of you in Joshua 1:8, are you guaranteed prosperity? **No.**

7. Write an essay describing what you hope your lifestyle will be like as an adult. How will you pay for it, and how will it honor the Lord?

Go For It! Examination
Chapter 10

1. Write this chapter's **Memorize It!** Scripture, Philippians 4:11-13.

2. Define contentment.

3. Describe how a person can learn to be content.

4. Why should godly people not worry or be envious of the wicked who become prosperous?

5. Read Joshua 1:8. According to this passage, what must you do to put yourself in a position to experience prosperity?

6. If you are faithful to do all that is required of you in Joshua 1:8, are you guaranteed prosperity?

7. Write an essay describing what you hope your lifestyle will be like as an adult. How will you pay for it, and how will it honor the Lord?

Prayer Logs

"Pray for one another" (JAMES 5:16).

Name _____   Parents _____

Home phone _____   Brothers and Sisters _____

Cell phone _____   _____

E-mail _____   _____

Home address _____   _____

_____   _____

WEEK	PRAYER REQUEST(S)	ANSWERS TO PRAYER
1		
2		
3		
4		
5		
6		
7		
8		
9		
10	My long-term prayer request:	

"Pray for one another" (JAMES 5:16).

Name _____

Home phone _____

Cell phone _____

E-mail _____

Home address _____

_____

Parents _____

Brothers and Sisters _____

_____

_____

_____

WEEK	PRAYER REQUEST(S)	ANSWERS TO PRAYER
1		
2		
3		
4		
5		
6		
7		
8		
9		
10	My long-term prayer request:	

"Pray for one another" (JAMES 5:16).

Name _____   Parents _____

Home phone _____   Brothers and Sisters _____

Cell phone _____   _____

E-mail _____   _____

Home address _____   _____

_____   _____

WEEK	PRAYER REQUEST(S)	ANSWERS TO PRAYER
1		
2		
3		
4		
5		
6		
7		
8		
9		
10	My long-term prayer request:	

"Pray for one another" (JAMES 5:16).

Name _____   Parents _____

Home phone _____   Brothers and Sisters _____

Cell phone _____   _____

E-mail _____   _____

Home address _____   _____

_____   _____

WEEK	PRAYER REQUEST(S)	ANSWERS TO PRAYER
1		
2		
3		
4		
5		
6		
7		
8		
9		
10	My long-term prayer request:	

"Pray for one another" (James 5:16).

Name _____   Parents _____

Home phone _____   Brothers and Sisters _____

Cell phone _____   _____

E-mail _____   _____

Home address _____   _____

_____   _____

Week	Prayer Request(s)	Answers to Prayer
1		
2		
3		
4		
5		
6		
7		
8		
9		
10	My long-term prayer request:	

"Pray for one another" (JAMES 5:16).

Name _____   Parents _____

Home phone _____   Brothers and Sisters _____

Cell phone _____   _____

E-mail _____   _____

Home address _____   _____

_____   _____

WEEK	PRAYER REQUEST(S)	ANSWERS TO PRAYER
1		
2		
3		
4		
5		
6		
7		
8		
9		
10	My long-term prayer request:	

"Pray for one another" (JAMES 5:16).

Name _____

Home phone _____

Cell phone _____

E-mail _____

Home address _____

_____

Parents _____

Brothers and Sisters _____

_____

_____

_____

WEEK	PRAYER REQUEST(S)	ANSWERS TO PRAYER
1		
2		
3		
4		
5		
6		
7		
8		
9		
10	My long-term prayer request:	

"Pray for one another" (JAMES 5:16).

Name _____ Parents _____

Home phone _____ Brothers and Sisters _____

Cell phone _____ _____

E-mail _____ _____

Home address _____ _____

_____ _____

WEEK	PRAYER REQUEST(S)	ANSWERS TO PRAYER
1		
2		
3		
4		
5		
6		
7		
8		
9		
10	My long-term prayer request:	

"Pray for one another" (JAMES 5:16).

Name _____   Parents _____

Home phone _____   Brothers and Sisters _____

Cell phone _____   _____

E-mail _____   _____

Home address _____   _____

_____   _____

WEEK	PRAYER REQUEST(S)	ANSWERS TO PRAYER
1		
2		
3		
4		
5		
6		
7		
8		
9		
10	My long-term prayer request:	

"Pray for one another" (JAMES 5:16).

Name _____   Parents _____

Home phone _____   Brothers and Sisters _____

Cell phone _____   _____

E-mail _____   _____

Home address _____   _____

_____   _____

WEEK	PRAYER REQUEST(S)	ANSWERS TO PRAYER
1		
2		
3		
4		
5		
6		
7		
8		
9		
10	My long-term prayer request:	

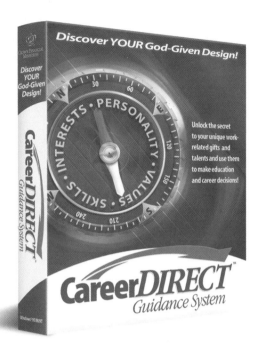